vietnamese

vietnamese

nguyen thanh diep

Marshall Cavendish
Cuisine

Editor: Lydia Leong
Designer: Bernard Go Kwang Meng

This book contains previously published material from Feast of Flavours from the Vietnamese Kitchen

Published by Marshall Cavendish Cuisine
An imprint of Marshall Cavendish International
1 New Industrial Road, Singapore 536196

Other Marshall Cavendish Offices:
Marshall Cavendish Ltd. 119 Wardour Street, London W1F 0UW, UK • Marshall Cavendish Corporation. 99 White Plains
Road, Tarrytown NY 10591-9001, USA • Marshall Cavendish International (Thailand) Co Ltd. 253 Asoke, 12th Flr,
Sukhumvit 21 Road, Klongtoey Nua, Wattana, Bangkok 10110, Thailand • Marshall Cavendish (Malaysia) Sdn Bhd,
Times Subang, Lot 46, Subang Hi-Tech Industrial Park, Batu Tiga, 40000 Shah Alam, Selangor Darul Ehsan, Malaysia

Marshall Cavendish is a trademark of Times Publishing Limited

National Library Board Singapore Cataloguing in Publication Data

Nguyen Thanh Diep.
Vietnamese / Nguyen Thanh Diep. – Singapore : Marshall Cavendish Cuisine, c2008.
p. cm. – (Mini cookbooks)
ISBN-13 : 978-981-261-562-6
ISBN-10 : 981-261-562-8

1. Cookery, Vietnamese. I. Title. II. Series: Mini cookbooks

TX724.5.V5
641.59597 -- dc22   OCN183180051

Printed in Singapore by Saik Wah Press Pte Ltd

contents

vietnamese

fresh spring rolls Makes about 30

The combination of Chinese lettuce, mint leaves and garlic chives gives this Vietnamese classic an unmistakably light and fresh taste.

INGREDIENTS

Round rice papers	30 sheets, each 20 cm (8 in) in diameter
Chinese lettuce leaves	300 g (11 oz), washed and drained
Mint leaves	50 g (1³/₄ oz), washed and stalks discarded
Fresh rice vermicelli	1 kg (2 lb 3 oz)
Garlic (Chinese) chives	200 g (7 oz), washed and cut into 12-cm (5-in) lengths
Lean pork	300 g (11 oz), boiled for 15 minutes, or until cooked, then cut into 30 thin slices
Freshwater prawns (shrimps)	500 g (1 lb 1¹/₂ oz), boiled and peeled

DIPPING SAUCE (COMBINED)

Preserved soy bean paste	5 Tbsp
Coconut juice	2 Tbsp
Chopped lemon grass	1 Tbsp
Light soy sauce	1 Tbsp
Skinned peanuts	2 Tbsp, pounded
Sugar	2 tsp
Minced chilli	2 tsp
Minced garlic	2 tsp

NOTE
Indian string hoppers (putu mayam) or thick round rice (laksa) noodles can be used in place of fresh rice vermicelli in this recipe.

METHOD

- Lay a sheet of rice paper on a tray or plate. Smear on warm, boiled water to soften. Place a lettuce leaf and mint leaf at the lower end of rice paper, followed by some rice vermicelli. Fold left and right sides of rice paper over filling. The resulting length should be about 10 cm (4 in).

- Position a chive stalk along length of roll, leaving about 2 cm (1 in) to stick out on one side. Put a slice of pork and 2 prawns on top of other ingredients, then roll up firmly. Dampened rice paper will stick and be sealed. Repeat process until ingredients are used up.

- Combine ingredients for dipping sauce in a bowl. Serve rolls with dipping sauce.

deep-fried spring rolls Makes about 30

This Vietnamese fried spring roll is richly stuffed with pork, crabmeat, yam and wood ear fungus.

INGREDIENTS

Minced pork	300 g (11 oz)
Crabmeat	300 g (11 oz), coarsely chopped and mashed, or minced prawn (shrimp) meat
Yam (taro)	300 g (11 oz), peeled and finely shredded
Dried wood ear fungus	5 pieces, soaked to soften, hard stems trimmed and discarded, and finely shredded
Minced shallots	2 tsp
Minced garlic	1 tsp
Round rice papers	30 sheets, each 15 cm (6 in) in diameter
Coconut juice	125 ml (4 fl oz / $^1/_2$ cup)
Cooking oil	500 ml (16 fl oz / 2 cups)
Chinese lettuce and mint leaves	

SEASONING

Chicken seasoning powder	4 tsp
Ground black pepper	1 tsp
Salt	2 tsp

DIPPING SAUCE (COMBINED)

Fish sauce	1 Tbsp
Coconut juice	2 Tbsp, or boiled water
Sugar	1 tsp
Vinegar	1 Tbsp, or lemon juice
Garlic	1 clove, peeled and minced
Red chilli (optional)	1, or to taste, minced

METHOD

- Prepare stuffing. Combine pork, crabmeat, yam, fungus, shallots and garlic in a large bowl. Add seasoning and mix well.

- Lay a sheet of rice paper on a tray. Smear on coconut juice to soften. Spoon 1 Tbsp stuffing onto lower end of rice paper, then fold in left and right sides and roll up firmly. Each roll should be 3–4 cm (1 1/2–2 in) long. Repeat until ingredients are used up.

- Heat oil and deep-fry spring rolls in batches over medium heat until golden brown. Remove and drain well.

- Combine ingredients for dipping sauce in a bowl.

- Serve spring rolls hot, with lettuce, mint leaves and dipping sauce.

hanoi prawn fritters Makes 25–30

Traditionally, prawns for the dish were not peeled because of the calcium the shells contained.
The shells also help maintain crispness.

INGREDIENTS

Limes	as required
Water	as required
Potatoes	500 g (1 lb 1 1/2 oz), peeled and julienned
Prawns (shrimps)	1 kg (2 lb 3 oz), small (50–60 pieces), peeled, if desired, leaving tails intact
Cooking oil	500 ml (16 fl oz / 2 cups)

BATTER

Eggs	3
Plain (all-purpose) flour	500 g (1 lb 1 1/2 oz)
Rice flour	250 g (9 oz)
Ground turmeric	2 tsp
Chicken seasoning powder	4 tsp
Salt	2 tsp
Hot water	as required

DIPPING SAUCE (COMBINED)

Fish sauce	1 Tbsp
Coconut juice	2 Tbsp, or boiled water
Sugar	1 tsp
Vinegar	1 Tbsp, or lemon juice
Garlic	1 clove, peeled and minced
Red chilli (optional)	1, or to taste, minced

METHOD

- Make sufficient lime water to soak julienned potatoes until required. To make lime water, squeeze the juice of 1 lime into 1 litre (32 fl oz / 4 cups) water, increasing proportionately.

- Prepare batter. In a bowl, beat eggs, then mix in plain and rice flours. Add turmeric, seasoning powder and salt, then continue to beat until mixture is smooth. Add some hot water if the mixture is too thick.

- Combine batter, prawns and drained julienned potatoes in a large bowl.

- Heat oil in a wok or frying pan. Use a ladle to scoop batter (containing at least 2 prawns and some potato shreds) and lower into hot oil. Make sure fritters do not stick together while frying. Cook until golden brown. Drain well.

- Combine ingredients for dipping sauce in a bowl.

- Serve fritters with dipping sauce. For a lighter experience, enjoy fritters with lettuce and mint leaves.

prawn paste on sugar cane   Makes about 20

Juicy prawn meat on lengths of sweet sugar cane are bound to delight whenever this is served.

INGREDIENTS

Sugar cane	5 sticks, each 10-cm (4-in) long, washed and peeled
Lard	100 g (3$^1/_2$ oz), washed and cut into 1.5-cm ($^3/_4$-in) wide pieces
Sugar	3 tsp
Prawns (shrimps)	1 kg (2 lb 3 oz), peeled and deveined
Garlic	10 cloves, peeled
Salt	1 tsp

DIPPING SAUCE (COMBINED)

Fish sauce	1 Tbsp
Coconut juice	2 Tbsp, or boiled water
Sugar	1 tsp
Vinegar	1 Tbsp, or lemon juice
Garlic	1 clove, peeled and minced
Red chilli (optional)	1, or to taste, minced

METHOD

• Quarter each sugar cane piece lengthways, then pare the edge down to make rounder.

• Combine lard and sugar in an ovenproof bowl, then leave in oven preheated to 120°C (250°F) for about 30 minutes.

• Blend prawns and garlic together until well mixed. Combine with lard and sugar, then add salt. Take 1 Tbsp paste and press around central portion of a sugar cane length, covering roughly two-thirds of stick. Repeat until ingredients are used up.

• Deep-fry, barbecue or oven grill prepared sugar cane lengths.

• Combine ingredients for dipping sauce in a bowl.

• Serve prawn paste with dipping sauce or bottled chilli sauce.

beef rolls Makes 25–30

Deeply aromatic and rich with meat juices, this starter will please any meat-lover.

INGREDIENTS

Beef fillet	I kg (2 lb 3 oz)
Brandy	I tsp
Lean pork or chicken breast	450 g (I lb), minced
Crabmeat	100 g (3¹/₂ oz)
Straw mushrooms	200 g (7 oz), finely chopped
Cooking oil	2 Tbsp
Chinese lettuce leaves	300 g (I I oz), washed and drained

SEASONING

Chicken seasoning powder	4 tsp
Ground white pepper	I tsp
Salt	I tsp

DIPPING SAUCE (COMBINED)

Fish sauce	I Tbsp
Coconut juice	2 Tbsp, or boiled water
Sugar	I tsp
Vinegar	I Tbsp, or lemon juice
Garlic	I clove, peeled and minced
Red chilli (optional)	I, or to taste, minced

METHOD

- Cut beef into thin slices, about 3 x 6 cm (1 1/2 x 3 in). When done, put beef slices in a bowl and add brandy. Mix and set aside for 30 minutes.

- Prepare filling. Combine minced pork or chicken, crabmeat and mushrooms in a bowl. Mix in seasoning and set aside.

- Heat cooking oil in a frying pan. Add filling and stir-fry for 10 minutes, or until meat is cooked. Dish out and leave to cool for about 10 minutes.

- Put about 2 tsp filling onto a beef slice and roll up firmly. Repeat until beef slices are used up.

- Poke 3–4 rolls onto a skewer and grill over charcoal heat. The rolls should be cooked after 10 minutes of grilling, or when they turn golden on the outside. Alternatively, bake in an oven preheated to 160°C (325°F) for about 8 minutes, turning once or twice.

- Combine ingredients for dipping sauce in a bowl.

- Remove rolls from skewers and arrange on a serving plate with lettuce. To eat, wrap a beef roll with a lettuce leaf, then dip into sauce.

fried chicken wings in fish sauce Serves 4–5

A favourite of many, deep-fried chicken wings are given a Vietnamese twist in this recipe.

INGREDIENTS

Chicken wings	1 kg (2 lb 3 oz), washed and each cut into 2 pieces
Minced garlic	3 tsp
Chicken seasoning powder	3 tsp
Salt	1/2 tsp
Cooking oil	500 ml (16 fl oz / 2 cups)
Fish sauce	125 ml (4 fl oz / 1/2 cup)
Sugar	1 1/2 Tbsp

DIPPING SAUCE (COMBINED)

Lime juice	1 Tbsp
Salt	2 tsp
Ground black pepper	1 tsp

METHOD

• Season chicken wings with minced garlic, seasoning powder and salt. Set aside for 30 minutes.

• Heat oil in a wok or deep-fryer. Lower chicken wings into hot oil and deep-fry over medium heat until golden brown. Remove and drain well.

• In a wok or cooking pan, cook fish sauce and sugar over low heat until sugar is completely melted and liquid thickens. Add fried chicken wings and mix to coat wings well with sauce. Remove from heat to a serving plate.

• Combine ingredients for dipping sauce in a bowl.

• Serve chicken wings with dipping sauce.

squid cakes Serves 4–5

Similar to fish cakes, but much tastier, especially when eaten with lettuce and mint leaves and a sweet and sour dipping sauce.

INGREDIENTS

Squid	I kg (2 lb 3 oz), washed, cleaned and skinned
Minced garlic	$^1/_2$ tsp
Minced shallot	I tsp
Green (mung) bean powder	$^1/_2$ tsp
Cooking oil	125 ml (4 fl oz / $^1/_2$ cup)
Chinese lettuce leaves	200 g (7 oz), washed and drained
Mint leaves	as required

SEASONING

Chicken seasoning powder	3 tsp
Ground white pepper	I tsp
Sugar	I tsp
Salt	I tsp

DIPPING SAUCE (COMBINED)

Fish sauce	I Tbsp
Coconut juice	2 Tbsp, or boiled water
Sugar	I tsp
Vinegar	I Tbsp, or lemon juice
Garlic	I clove, peeled and minced
Red chilli (optional)	I, or to taste, minced

METHOD

- Cut squid tubes into small pieces, then blend to a fine paste. Transfer to a mixing bowl and season with minced garlic and shallot, as well as seasoning ingredients. Mix well.

- Shape squid paste into balls about 5 cm (2 in) in diameter. Flatten into round patties about 0.5-cm ($^1/_4$-in) thick.

- Heat oil in a wok or frying pan and cook squid patties until golden brown.

- Cut squid cakes into diamond shapes and arrange on a plate. Garnish as desired.

- Combine ingredients for dipping sauce in a bowl.

- Serve squid cakes with lettuce and mint leaves, as well as dipping sauce.

pumpkin soup with coconut milk Serves 4–5

Sweet pumpkin, creamy coconut milk, and tiny but pungent dried prawns combine to produce a
richly flavoured soup.

INGREDIENTS

Coconut milk	300 ml (10 fl oz / 1 1/4 cups)
Water	800 ml (26 fl oz / 3 1/4 cups)
Dried prawns (shrimps)	50 g (1 3/4 oz), soaked in warm water for 15 minutes, then drained and roughly pounded
Pumpkin	1 kg (2 lb 3 oz), peeled and cut into bite-size pieces
Straw mushrooms	300 g (11 oz)
Soft bean curd	20 cubes, each 5-cm (2-in), deep-fried
Chicken seasoning powder	3 tsp
Salt	2 tsp
Ground black pepper	2 tsp

METHOD

- Bring coconut milk and water to the boil in a pot. Add dried prawns and pumpkin pieces. Cook for 10 minutes over medium heat.

- Add mushrooms and fried bean curd cubes. Cook for 5 minutes more, then stir in seasoning powder and salt.

- Transfer soup to a large serving bowl and sprinkle pepper over.

- Serve soup with steamed rice.

vietnamese sour fish soup Serves 4

Brightly colourful and appetisingly tangy, this nutritious soup of fish, pineapple and vegetables is full of crunch and a pleasure to the senses.

INGREDIENTS

Mackerel or mudfish (snakehead), or other freshwater fish	1, about 1 kg (2 lb 3 oz)
Pork stock	from boiling 300 g (11 oz) pork bones in 1 litre (32 fl oz / 4 cups) water for 1–2 hours
Salt	1 tsp, or to taste
Tamarind juice	from stirring 20 g (^{2}/$_3$ oz) tamarind pulp in 250 ml (8 fl oz / 1 cup) hot water and strained
Pineapple	^{1}/$_2$, peeled, quartered lengthways then cut across into 0.5-cm (^{1}/$_4$-in) thick slices
Tomatoes	2, each cut into 8 wedges
Bean sprouts	50 g (1^3/$_4$ oz), tailed
Chinese celery	50 g (1^3/$_4$ oz), leaves separated and stems cut into 3-cm (1^1/$_2$-in) lengths
Minced garlic	1 tsp, crisp-fried
Fish sauce	2 Tbsp
Red chilli slices	2 Tbsp

SEASONING

Chicken seasoning powder	^{1}/$_2$ tsp
Fish sauce	^{1}/$_2$ tsp
Sugar	^{1}/$_2$ tsp

METHOD

- Wash and clean fish. Make 3 diagonal cuts on each side of body. Set aside.

- Bring stock to the boil. Season with salt. Add fish and allow liquid to return to the boil, then add tamarind juice. Regularly remove scum from liquid surface.

- When fish is almost cooked, add seasoning. The soup should taste sour and sweet. Adjust to taste, then add pineapple and tomatoes, bean sprouts and Chinese celery stems. Return liquid to the boil before removing from heat.

- Transfer all or a portion of fish soup to a serving bowl, then garnish with fried garlic and Chinese celery leaves.

- Serve fish soup with fish sauce in a small saucer and chilli slices in another.

green mango salad Serves 4–6

Also known as Vietnamese mint, polygonum leaves impart an intense and inimitable aroma that brings out the flavour of prawns.

INGREDIENTS

Green mangoes	1 kg (2 lb 3 oz), peeled, seeded and julienned
Prawns (shrimps)	300 g (11 oz), barbecued or grilled, then peeled, leaving tails intact
Polygonum (laksa) leaves	20 g ($^2/_3$ oz), stalks discarded and leaves coarsely chopped
Skinned peanuts	50 g (1$^3/_4$ oz), roasted and coarsely pounded
Prawn (shrimp) crackers	20, deep-fried

DRESSING (COMBINED)

Chilli sauce	4 Tbsp
Sugar	3 Tbsp, or more to taste
Light soy sauce	2 Tbsp

DIPPING SAUCE (COMBINED)

Fish sauce	1 Tbsp
Coconut juice	2 Tbsp, or boiled water
Sugar	1 tsp
Vinegar	1 Tbsp, or lemon juice
Garlic	1 clove, peeled and minced
Red chilli (optional)	1, or to taste, minced

METHOD

- Combine ingredients for dressing in a large bowl. Add mango shreds and toss. Do not squeeze mango shreds or crispness will be lost. Adjust to taste with some sugar if mango is too sour.

- Transfer salad to a serving plate. Arrange prawns on top. Garnish with chopped polygonum leaves and pounded peanuts.

- Combine ingredients for dipping sauce in a bowl.

- Serve salad with prawn crackers and dipping sauce.

water convolvulus salad Serves 4–6

Water convolvulus, or water spinach, is very rich in iron. Paired with a basic Vietnamese salad dressing, it makes a nutritious yet tasty dish.

INGREDIENTS

Water convolvulus	1 kg (2 lb 3 oz), use stalks only
Salt	2 Tbsp
Sesame seed oil	2 tsp
Pork thigh	200 g (7 oz), with a bit of skin and fat intact, boiled and thinly sliced
Prawns (shrimps)	300 g (11 oz), boiled and peeled, leaving tails intact
Polygonum (laksa) leaves	20 g (²/₃ oz), stalks discarded and leaves coarsely chopped
Skinned peanuts	50 g (1³/₄ oz), roasted and coarsely pounded
Shallots	30 g (1 oz), peeled, sliced and crisp-fried

DRESSING

Sugar	6 Tbsp
Lime juice	6 Tbsp
Chicken seasoning powder	4 tsp
Fish sauce	2 Tbsp

DIPPING SAUCE (COMBINED)

Fish sauce	1 Tbsp
Coconut juice	2 Tbsp, or boiled water
Sugar	1 tsp
Vinegar	1 Tbsp, or lemon juice
Garlic	1 clove, peeled and minced
Red chilli (optional)	1, or to taste, minced

METHOD

- Cut water convolvulus stalks into 8-cm (3-in) lengths, then, halve each length lengthways. Add salt and knead for a few minutes to extract juice which tastes of tannins. Discard juice and rinse stalks well.

- Combine all dressing ingredients in a mixing bowl. Stir until sugar dissolves. Add stalks and toss together with sesame seed oil. Mix well.

- Transfer salad to a serving plate or bowl. Arrange pork slices and prawns on top.

- Combine ingredients for dipping sauce in a bowl.

- Garnish salad with polygonum leaves, peanuts and crisp-fried shallots. Serve with dipping sauce.

beef salad Serves 4–5

Star fruit slices make this salad refreshingly juicy, banana slices give it substance, while onion rings give bite and zing.

INGREDIENTS

Beef fillet	600 g (1 lb 5 oz)
Vinegar	as required
Water	as required
Raw green banana	1, peeled and thinly sliced
Raw star fruit	2, peeled and thinly sliced
Onions	2, peeled and cut into thin rings
Cooking oil	1–2 Tbsp
Coriander leaves (cilantro)	20 g (^{2}/$_3$ oz)
Skinned peanuts	50 g (1^3/$_4$ oz), roasted and coarsely pounded
Red chilli	1, finely sliced
Shallots	30 g (1 oz), peeled, sliced and crisp-fried
Prawn (shrimp) crackers	20, deep-fried

SEASONING

Chopped garlic	2 tsp, pan-fried in oil until golden brown
Ground black pepper	2 tsp
Sugar	2 tsp
Sesame seed oil	2 tsp

METHOD

- Slice beef thinly and across the grain to ensure tenderness. Put beef slices into a bowl. Add seasoning ingredients and mix well. Set aside for 10 minutes.

- Make sufficient vinegar-water mixture (3 parts water to 1 part vinegar) to soak cut banana, star fruit and onion rings separately.

- Heat oil in a frying pan over high heat for 30 seconds. Add beef slices and stir-fry quickly, then remove from heat.

- Drain all soaked ingredients well, then combine with cooked beef in a mixing bowl and toss. Transfer to a serving dish.

- Garnish with coriander leaves, peanuts, chilli and crisp-fried shallots. Serve with prawn crackers and dipping sauce (page 30).

chicken salad with polygonum leaves Serves 4–6

A tangy and peppery salad of tender chicken, aromatic polygonum leaves and crisp onion strips will whet any sluggish appetite.

INGREDIENTS

Vinegar	as required
Water	as required
Onions	2, peeled and cut into half-moon slices
Chicken	1, whole, 1.5–2 kg (3 lb 4$^1/_2$ oz–4 lb 6 oz)
Rice wine or vodka	3 Tbsp
Polygonum (laksa) leaves	50 g (1$^3/_4$ oz), stalks discarded
Red chillies	1–2, sliced

SEASONING

Ground black pepper	1 tsp
Chicken seasoning powder	3 tsp
Sugar	1$^1/_2$ Tbsp
Salt	2 tsp
Lime juice	3 Tbsp

DIPPING SAUCE (COMBINED)

Lime juice	1 Tbsp
Salt	2 tsp
Ground black pepper	1 tsp

METHOD

- Make sufficient vinegar-water mixture to soak onion slices. To make water-vinegar mixture, mix 3 parts water with 1 part vinegar. Drain onion slices well before use.

- Steam chicken for 20 minutes, or until cooked through. Remove chicken from steamer and sprinkle rice wine or vodka over. Return chicken to steamer and replace lid. Leave for 5 minutes, then remove from heat.

- Debone slightly cooled chicken and cut flesh into desired bite-size pieces. Alternatively, shred chicken meat by hand.

- Put chicken into a mixing bowl. Add polygonum leaves, drained onion slices and seasoning. Mix well. Transfer salad to a serving dish.

- Combine ingredients for dipping sauce in a bowl.

- Garnish salad with chilli, then serve with dipping sauce.

fish and pineapple stew Serves 4–6

Tangy pineapple slices tame the pungent taste of fish sauce in this dish, while the bird's eye chillies impart fiery spiciness.

INGREDIENTS

Tuna	I kg (2 lb 3 oz), cut into I-cm ($^1/_2$-in) thick pieces
Minced garlic	2 tsp
Chicken seasoning powder	3 tsp
Ground black pepper	I tsp
Cooking oil	5 Tbsp
Pineapple	I, peeled, quartered lengthways, cored and cut into 0.5-cm ($^1/_4$-in) thick slices
Bird's eye chillies	5, halved
Fish sauce	4 Tbsp, or more to taste
Coconut juice	500 ml (16 fl oz / 2 cups)

METHOD

• Season fish with garlic, seasoning powder and pepper. Set aside for 30 minutes to I hour.

• Heat oil in a frying pan. Add seasoned fish and cook until golden brown. Dish out and set aside.

• Use a clay or heavy-based pot to stew. Arrange a layer of pineapple pieces to cover base of vessel, followed by a layer of fish on top. Arrange a second layer of pineapple atop fish, followed by a second layer of fish. Repeat to layer ingredients until the 2 ingredients are used up. Chillies will be placed last and right on top.

• Pour in fish sauce and coconut juice to cover ingredients. Simmer over low heat for 30 minutes or until liquid thickens.

• Garnish as desired before serving.

baked crabs Makes 3

Crab top shells filled with juicy, creamy crabmeat and sealed with golden breadcrumb crusts
make a great meal and talking point.

INGREDIENTS

Milk	250 ml (8 fl oz / 1 cup)
Bread	2 slices, crusts discarded and torn into small pieces
Butter	50 g (1$^3/_4$ oz)
Minced garlic	1 tsp
Minced shallot	1 tsp
Crabs	3, about 1 kg (2 lb 3 oz), washed, steamed until cooked, top shells and grey crab curd on underside reserved and meat extracted
Dried breadcrumbs	20 g ($^2/_3$ oz)

SEASONING

Ground black pepper	$^1/_4$ tsp
Salt	1 tsp
Chicken seasoning powder	1 tsp

METHOD

- Combine milk and bread in a bowl. Leave to soak for 15 minutes or until bread is soft and soggy. Squeeze out and discard about half the milk. Mash bread to achieve a soft, smooth paste.

- Heat butter in a wok or frying pan. Add garlic and shallot and fry until fragrant. Add crab curd and crabmeat and fry for 5–10 minutes before removing from heat.

- Mix cooked crabmeat and milk-soaked bread together, then add seasoning. Adjust to taste if necessary.

- Stuff each top shell with crabmeat mixture, then sprinkle breadcrumbs over to cover surface. Place on a baking tray.

- Bake crab shells in an oven preheated to 350°C (662°F) for about 5 minutes, or until surface is golden brown.

- Garnish as desired and serve.

steamed fish with fermented soy beans

Serves 4–6

Laden with complementary ingredients, the fish here is only half the show, and the soy bean paste is what holds all the flavours together.

INGREDIENTS

Garoupa, red snapper or sea bass	1, whole, about 1 kg (2 lb 3 oz), cleaned
Salt	1 Tbsp
Cooking oil	as required
Glass vermicelli	10 g (1/3 oz), cut into 5-cm (2-in) lengths, then soaked in water to soften
Dried wood ear fungus	5 g (1/6 oz), soaked in water to soften, then shredded
Chinese cabbage	1 head, about 500 g (1 lb 1 1/2 oz), cut into 5-cm (2-in) wide diamond-shaped pieces
Tomatoes	2, each cut into 6 wedges
Ginger (optional)	1–2-cm (1/2–1-in) knob, peeled and julienned
Onion	1, peeled and cut into wedges
Preserved soy bean paste	100 g (3 1/2 oz)
Red chilli	1, sliced
Coriander leaves (cilantro)	

SEASONING (COMBINED)

Light soy sauce	1 tsp
Sugar	1 tsp
Ground white pepper	1 tsp

METHOD

- Rub fish all over with salt. Heat some oil and pan-fry fish until slightly golden. Transfer fish to a large heatproof serving plate.

- Evenly distribute all remaining ingredient, except coriander leaves over and around fish. Pour combined seasoning over fish.

- Steam until cooked, then garnish with coriander leaves. Serve hot.

stir-fried minced eel with lemon grass Serves 4–5

The spicy and aromatic combination of onions, garlic, lemon grass and chillies remove any hint of fishiness from this dish.

INGREDIENTS

Eels	2, washed and deboned
Lard	50 g (1³/₄ oz)
Onions	50 g (1³/₄ oz), peeled and minced
Garlic	50 g (1³/₄ oz), peeled and minced
Cooking oil	125 ml (4 fl oz / ¹/₂ cup)
Minced lemon grass	3 tsp
Minced red chillies	3 tsp
Fish sauce	1 tsp
Skinned peanuts	50 g (1³/₄ oz), roasted and coarsely pounded
Sesame crackers	20, about 30-cm (12-in) wide, deep-fried, or use papadums or prawn crackers

SEASONING

Salt	¹/₂ tsp
Sugar	¹/₂ tsp
Chicken seasoning powder	¹/₂ tsp

METHOD

- Chop eels, lard, onions and garlic together until well minced. Mix in seasoning ingredients.

- Heat oil in a pan or wok. Fry lemon grass and chillies until golden brown. Add chopped eel mixture and stir-fry until cooked. Season with fish sauce, then dish out.

- Sprinkle roasted peanuts on top and garnish as desired.

- Use crackers as an edible spoon to scoop up cooked ingredients.

fried crab in tamarind sauce Serves 4

A quaint rendition of the sweet-and-sour formula, this crab dish has a delightfully balanced and appetising flavour.

INGREDIENTS

Cooking oil	500 ml (16 fl oz / 2 cups)
Crab(s)	1–2, about 1 kg (2 lb 3 oz), washed, top shell(s) and grey crab curd underside reserved, pincers separated and cracked and remaining crab quartered
Onion	1, peeled and cut into wedges
Minced garlic	2 tsp
Minced shallots	2 tsp
Tamarind pulp	50 g (1³/₄ oz), soaked in root beer or sarsaparilla (sarsi) and drained before use
Root beer or sarsaparilla	250 ml (8 fl oz / 1 cup)
Watercress	100 g (3¹/₂ oz)
French loaf	1

SEASONING

Salt	¹/₄ tsp
Ground black pepper	¹/₄ tsp
Sugar	¹/₄ tsp
Chicken seasoning powder	¹/₄ tsp, or to taste

DIPPING SAUCE (COMBINED)

Lime juice	1 Tbsp
Salt	2 tsp
Ground black pepper	1 tsp

METHOD

- Heat oil in a wok. Add crab pincers and fry for 4 minutes, then add crab quarters and cook for 5 minutes. Lastly, add top shell(s) and cook for 3 minutes. Drain and set aside.

- Remove bulk of oil, leaving about 4 Tbsp in wok. Add onion wedges and stir-fry briefly, then dish out and set aside.

- Using the same oil, stir-fry garlic and shallots until fragrant. Add tamarind pulp, root beer or sarsaparilla and fried onion wedges. Cook over medium heat until liquid comes to the boil.

- Add crab pieces and cover with lid to cook. Stir occasionally.

- When liquid has thickened, add crab curd and mix well. Add seasoning and adjust to taste if necessary. Dish out to a serving bowl.

- Combine ingredients for dipping sauce in a bowl.

- Serve crab(s) with watercress, French loaf and dipping sauce.

prawns sautéed with pork belly Serves 4–5

Plain steamed rice best brings out the tastes and textures of this richly flavourful dish.

INGREDIENTS

Freshwater prawns (shrimps)	300 g (11 oz), washed and trimmed of feelers and sharp tips of heads
Pork belly	300 g (11 oz), washed and sliced
Salt	1 tsp
Chicken seasoning powder	2 tsp
Cooking oil	1 Tbsp
Minced garlic	1 tsp
Cucumber	1, sliced

SEASONING INGREDIENTS

Sugar	1 tsp
Fish sauce	1 Tbsp
Chilli powder	1 tsp

METHOD

- Season prawns and pork slices with salt and seasoning powder. Set aside.

- Heat cooking oil in a wok. Add garlic and stir-fry until fragrant. Add prawns and pork and sauté for 5 minutes, or until just cooked.

- Add seasoning and sauté for a few minutes more, until liquid is much reduced. Remove from heat and transfer to a serving plate.

- Serve with cucumber slices on the side.

stuffed squid Serves 4–6

This versatile dish can be one of several dishes served at a meal, a starter or a tasty afternoon snack.

INGREDIENTS

Pork	100 g (3^1/$_2$ oz)
Prawns (shrimps)	200 g (7 oz), peeled and deveined
Minced onion	1 tsp
Minced garlic	1 tsp
Salt	1 tsp
Chicken seasoning powder	2 tsp
Squid	500 g (1 lb 1^1/$_2$ oz), heads separated, quill discarded, tubes washed and skinned
Cooking oil	2 Tbsp + enough for deep-frying
Minced shallot	1 tsp
Tomato sauce (ketchup)	3 Tbsp
Ground black pepper	1 tsp
Sugar	^{1}/$_2$ tsp
Egg	1
Plain (all-purpose) flour	100 g (3^1/$_2$ oz)
Iceberg or Chinese lettuce	about 20 leaves, separated and washed
Chilli sauce	as required

METHOD

- Cut pork and peeled prawns into smaller pieces, then, blend together with onion and garlic until pasty. Transfer paste to a bowl.

- Season paste with $^1/_2$ tsp salt and 1 tsp seasoning powder. Mix well and stuff mixture into squid tubes. Sew up open ends with needle and thread to secure filling.

- Heat 2 Tbsp oil in a wok. Fry shallot until fragrant, then add tomato sauce and stir well. Remove sauce from heat and season with remaining salt and seasoning powder, as well as pepper and sugar. Set aside.

- Beat egg well. Dip squid in beaten egg, then coat with flour.

- Heat sufficient oil in a clean wok for deep-frying, then cook coated, stuffed squids until done.

- Arrange lettuce and cooked squid on serving plate. Pour prepared sauce over and serve with chilli sauce.

fried lemon grass chicken Serves 4–6

In this recipe, chicken pieces are dyed bright yellow by turmeric and flavoured by aromatic lemon grass and garlic.

INGREDIENTS

Chicken pieces	I kg (2 lb 3 oz), cut into bite-size pieces
Cooking oil	125 ml (4 fl oz / ¹/₂ cup)
Minced garlic	I tsp

MARINADE (COMBINED)

Minced lemon grass	3 Tbsp, use hard stalk only; bruise to release fragrance before mincing
Chicken seasoning powder	3 tsp
Ground turmeric	¹/₂ tsp
Minced red chilli	I tsp
Salt	2 tsp

METHOD

- Combine ingredients for marinade in a large bowl. Add chicken and mix well, then leave for 30 minutes to I hour.

- Heat oil in a frying pan until hot, then add garlic and fry until fragrant. Add marinated chicken and cook until golden brown.

- Dish out and garnish as desired. Serve with plain white rice.

steamed minced pork with duck eggs Serves 4

A dish with Chinese roots, this Vietnamese version differs in using duck eggs, as well as transparent vermicelli and dried wood ear fungus for added texture.

INGREDIENTS

Cooking oil	1 tsp
Garlic	1 clove, peeled and minced
Minced lean pork	300 g (11 oz)
Transparent (glass) vermicelli	5 g ($^1/_6$ oz), soaked in water for 10 minutes, then drained and cut into 1-cm ($^1/_2$-in) lengths
Dried wood ear fungus	3 pieces, soaked to soften, hard stems trimmed and discarded
Duck eggs	3, lightly beaten
Light soy sauce	2 Tbsp
Red chilli	1, sliced

SEASONING

Ground black pepper	1 tsp
Sugar	1 tsp
Salt	$^1/_2$ tsp
Cooking oil	1 tsp

METHOD

• Heat oil in a saucepan. Add garlic and fry until golden brown. Dish out and set aside.

• Combine minced pork, vermicelli, fungus, eggs and fried garlic in a heatproof bowl. Mix well. Add seasoning and mix well again.

• Place bowl in a steamer and steam over high heat for 30 minutes.

• Remove from steamer and serve directly from steaming bowl, with soy sauce and chilli slices on the side.

pork stewed in coconut juice Serves 4

Aside from tender and smooth pork pieces, the hardboiled eggs, in having absorbed the flavours of the gravy, also make tasty nourishment.

INGREDIENTS

Pork thigh	1 kg (2 lb 3 oz), with some skin and fat intact
Eggs	4
Coconut juice	1 litre (32 fl oz / 4 cups)

MARINADE (COMBINED)

Fish sauce	125 ml (4 fl oz / $^1/_2$ cup)
Salt (optional)	$^1/_2$ Tbsp
Brown sugar	4 tsp
Minced garlic	2 tsp

METHOD

• Wash and cut pork into bite-size pieces.

• Combine ingredients for marinade in a bowl. Add pork and mix well. Leave for 1 hour.

• Meanwhile, prepare hardboiled eggs. When eggs are cooked, transfer to a bowl of room-temperature water to cool, then peel and set aside.

• Transfer pork and marinade to a pot and cook until liquid is almost dried up. Stir occasionally.

• Add coconut juice and hardboiled eggs. Return to the boil, all the while skimming scum from liquid surface to keep gravy clear. When liquid reaches the boil, reduce heat and simmer until pork is lightly golden.

• When done, pork should be tender but not too soft; fat and skin would have separated a little from meat.

• Dish out and serve hot.

stir-fried frog in coconut milk Serves 4

This dish looks like a curry, but the use of frog meat distinguishes it from curries of other cuisines.

INGREDIENTS

Frogs	1 kg (2 lb 3 oz), washed, skinned and legs separated from bodies
Cooking oil	1–2 Tbsp
Minced garlic	1 tsp
Preserved soy bean paste	2 tsp
Coconut milk	500 ml (16 fl oz / 2 cups)
Water	500 ml (16 fl oz / 2 cups)
Skinned peanuts	50 g (1³/₄ oz), roasted and roughly pounded
Fish sauce	2 Tbsp
Red chilli	1, sliced

SEASONING

Salt	to taste
Ground black pepper	to taste
Chicken seasoning powder	to taste

MARINADE (COMBINED)

Minced lemon grass	4 tsp
Curry powder	2 tsp
Five-spice powder	1 tsp
Sesame seed oil	1 tsp
Ground black pepper	1 tsp
Salt	2 tsp
Sugar	1 tsp
Chicken seasoning powder	1 tsp

METHOD

- Combine ingredients for marinade in a large bowl and add frog pieces. Mix well and leave for 30 minutes.

- Heat oil in a pan or wok. Add garlic and fry until golden brown. Add frog pieces and stir quickly.

- Add preserved soy bean paste, 125 ml (4 fl oz / ½ cup) coconut milk and water. Cover pan to cook frog pieces. When cooked through, add remaining coconut milk and bring to the boil. Adjust to taste with seasoning before removing from heat.

- Dish out and sprinkle peanuts over. Garnish as desired and serve with fish sauce and sliced chilli.

beef noodles Serves 4

This is a classic Vietnamese meal of beef and rice noodles in a clear soup that belies its richness.

INGREDIENTS

Beef thigh	400 g (14 oz), with some ligaments, washed and dried
Beef fillet	400 g (14 oz), washed and thinly sliced across grain
Thin flat rice noodles	2 kg (4 lb 6 oz)
Bean sprouts	200 g (7 oz), washed and drained
Spring onions (scallions)	2–3, finely chopped
Large onion	1, peeled and thinly sliced
Preserved soy bean paste	5 g ($^1/_6$ oz)
Chilli sauce	5 g ($^1/_6$ oz)
Limes	4, quartered

STOCK

Large onion	1, roasted until slightly burnt, peeled and lightly pounded
Ginger	5-cm (2-in) knob, roasted until slightly burnt, peeled and lightly pounded
Cinnamon sticks	2
Star anise	3
Beef bones	1 kg (2 lb 3 oz), washed, boiled and strained, or beef stock granules
Water	5 litres (8 pints / 20 cups)

SEASONING

Salt	$^1/_4$ tsp
Ground white pepper	$^1/_4$ tsp
Chicken seasoning powder	$^1/_4$ tsp

METHOD

- Prepare stock. Put roasted onion and ginger, cinnamon and star anise into a small cloth bag and tie up. Place in a large pot with beef bones and water. Bring to the boil, then lower heat and simmer for $2^1/_4$ hours. Regularly skim off scum from liquid surface to keep stock clear.

- Add beef thigh and simmer for 45 minutes, or until ligaments soften. Remove beef thigh and thinly slice when cooled.

- Strain stock and discard solid ingredients. Return liquid to the boil, then add seasoning. Lower heat and leave stock to simmer.

- Put desired amounts of noodles and bean sprouts for one serving into a wire mesh strainer and blanch in boiling water. Place into an individual serving bowl. Repeat to make as many servings as required.

- Arrange raw beef fillet slices, cooked beef thigh slices, spring onions and onion over noodles. Ladle boiling stock over. Raw beef will cook in heat of stock.

- Serve immediately, with small saucers of preserved soy bean paste, chilli sauce and lime quarters on the side.

duck noodle soup Serves 4

A hearty meal of duck pieces dusted with fried shallot and peanuts in a soupy bed of noodles.

INGREDIENTS

Duck	1, about 2 kg (4 lb 6 oz), neck and feet discarded, halved lengthways
Lime juice	1 Tbsp
Minced ginger	1 Tbsp
Minced garlic	1 Tbsp
Chicken seasoning powder	3 tsp, or more to taste
Chicken stock	2 litres (64 fl oz / 8 cups)
Dried or canned bamboo shoots	300 g (11 oz), soaked in water overnight and drained before use if dried and sliced if canned
Salt	to taste
Shallots	100 g (3¹/₂ oz), peeled, sliced and crisp-fried
Skinned peanuts	100 g (3¹/₂ oz), coarsely ground
Fresh rice vermicelli	2 kg (4 lb 6 oz)
Bean sprouts	300 g (11 oz)
Spring onions (scallions)	100 g (3¹/₂ oz), chopped
Polygonum (laksa) leaves	50 g (1³/₄ oz), stems discarded and leaves coarsely chopped

DIPPING SAUCE

Minced ginger	1 Tbsp
Minced garlic	2 tsp
Minced red chilli	1 tsp
Sugar	2 Tbsp
Lime juice	1 Tbsp
Fish sauce	1 Tbsp
Warm water	125 ml (4 fl oz / ¹/₂ cup)

N O T E

If fresh rice vermicelli is not available, use 500 g (1 lb 1¹/₂ oz) dried rice vermicelli. Soak in water to soften, then drain before use.

METHOD

- Rub duck with combined lime juice and ginger to remove any unpleasant smell. Wash duck, then drain and season with garlic and seasoning powder.

- Bring stock to the boil, then lower in duck. Leave to cook for 15–20 minutes, then drain and set aside.

- Add bamboo shoots to stock and return to the boil. Adjust to taste with more seasoning powder and salt if desired. Leave to simmer.

- Chop cooked duck into bite-size pieces and arrange on a plate. Sprinkle on some fried shallot slices and ground peanuts.

- Blanch noodles and bean sprouts, then transfer to individual serving bowls. Top with some duck pieces, fried shallot slices, chopped spring onions and polygonum leaves, then ladle boiling stock over.

- To make dipping sauce, pound garlic and ginger together, then transfer to a bowl. Add all remaining ingredients and mix well. Sauce should taste sweet, sour and salty.

- Serve noodles with dipping sauce on the side.

crabmeat noodle soup Serves 4

The sweetness of crabmeat is given centre stage in this soup noodle dish.

INGREDIENTS

Cooking oil	1 Tbsp
Chopped garlic	2 Tbsp
Crabmeat	300 g (11 oz)
Salt	$1/2$ tsp
Ground white pepper	$1/2$ tsp
Fresh or canned straw mushrooms	200 g (7 oz), sliced
Thick round rice (laksa) noodles	1.5 kg (3 lb 4$1/2$ oz)
Shallots	30 g (1 oz), peeled, sliced and crisp-fried
Spring onions (scallions)	50 g (1$3/4$ oz), chopped
Fish sauce	2 Tbsp
Red chilli	1, sliced
Limes	3, quartered

STOCK

Pork bones	1 kg (2 lb 3 oz), washed
White radish	1, peeled and sliced
Water	3 litres (96 fl oz / 12 cups)
Green (mung) bean flour	1 Tbsp

SEASONING

Chicken seasoning powder	$1/2$ tsp
Ground black pepper	$1/2$ tsp
Salt	$1/2$ tsp

METHOD

- Prepare stock. Boil pork bones and radish in water for I hour. Skim scum off regularly from liquid surface to get a clear stock. Strain stock and discard bones and radish. Add green bean flour to thicken stock, then add seasoning. Sustain liquid at the boil.

- Heat oil in a wok. Add I Tbsp garlic and stir-fry until fragrant. Add crabmeat and sauté for a few minutes. Season with salt and pepper, then dish out to a plate.

- Add remaining garlic to wok. When fragrant, add mushrooms and fry for a few minutes. Dish out.

- Put desired amount of noodles into individual serving bowls and top with crabmeat and straw mushrooms. Ladle boiling stock over, then sprinkle with crisp-fried shallots and spring onions.

- Serve hot with fish sauce, chilli slices and lime quarters on the side.

duck cooked in fermented bean curd Serves 4–6

Duck, fermented bean curd and coconut milk come together to spike the tongue in this dish.

INGREDIENTS

Duck	1 whole, about 2 kg (4 lb 6 oz)
Rice wine	2 Tbsp
Ginger	50 g (1 3/4 oz), peeled and pounded until fine
Coconut milk	400 ml (12 1/2 fl oz)
Water	500 ml (16 fl oz / 2 cups)
Yam (taro)	500 g (1 lb 1 1/2 oz), peeled and cut to bite-size pieces
Salt	1 pinch, or to taste
Chicken seasoning powder	1/2 tsp, or to taste
Steamed rice	1 kg (2 lb 3 oz), or fresh rice vermicelli
Water convolvulus	500 g (1 lb 1 1/2 oz), leaves separated and stems cut into 4-cm (1 1/2-in) lengths

MARINADE (COMBINED)

Ground black pepper	1/2 tsp
Salt	1 tsp
Oyster sauce	1 tsp
Red fermented bean curd	50 g (1 3/4 oz)
Sugar	1 Tbsp
Chopped garlic	1 Tbsp, fried until golden brown

DIPPING SAUCE

Red fermented bean curd	50 g (1 3/4 oz)
Sugar	3 tsp
Coarsely chopped garlic	1 Tbsp, fried until golden brown

METHOD

- Rub duck all over with rice wine and ginger combined. Set aside for 15 minutes, then rinse and drain. Chop duck into bite-size pieces. Place in a bowl with combined marinade. Mix well and leave for 15 minutes.

- Bring coconut milk and water to the boil. Add duck pieces and cook over low heat for 15 minutes. Add yam and simmer until soft.

- Meanwhile, prepare dipping sauce. Blend red fermented bean curd and sugar together until well combined. Stir in fried garlic and set aside.

- Adjust soup to taste with salt and seasoning powder. Sustain soup at a slow boil.

- To serve, spoon steamed rice into individual serving bowls. Blanch some greens in hot soup to add on top. Drain and add duck and yam pieces, then ladle on soup. Serve with dipping sauce on the side.

saigon fish congee Serves 4

The Vietnamese touch of adding yam cubes and green beans to Chinese fish congee provides for a nutty aroma and more complex texture.

INGREDIENTS

Mud fish, red snapper or sea bass	1.3 kg (2 lb 13 oz), washed
Water	2.5 litres (80 fl oz / 10 cups)
Fragrant rice	1 cup, washed and lightly roasted
Green (mung) beans	150 g (5 1/3 oz), soaked in water for 1 hour, or until softened; skins discarded
Yam (taro)	300 g (11 oz), peeled and cut into large cubes
Straw mushrooms	200 g (7 oz), sliced
Bean sprouts	200 g (7 oz)
Chopped spring onions (scallions)	3 Tbsp
Ginger	2-cm (1-in) knob, peeled and shredded
Ground black pepper	1/2 tsp

SEASONING

Crisp-fried shallots	4 tsp
Sesame seed oil	2 tsp
Salt	2 tsp
Chicken seasoning powder	3 tsp

METHOD

- Skin, bone and fillet fish. Reserve skin and bones for stock. Slice fillets and place in a bowl. Add seasoning, mix and set aside for 15 minutes.

- In a pot, combine fish skin and bones and water. Bring to the boil, then lower heat and simmer for 30 minutes. Strain stock and discard solid ingredients. Add rice to stock and cook for 1 hour until rice softens.

- Add green beans and yam. Simmer for 15 minutes. Add fish slices and mushrooms. Simmer for 5 minutes more, or until the fish is cooked through.

- Place bean sprouts into individual serving bowls. Ladle hot porridge over.

- Serve hot, topped with desired amounts of chopped spring onions, shredded ginger and ground black pepper.

quang noodles Serves 4

A satisfying meal of spicy pork slices and juicy prawns resting on a bed of yellow noodles and dusted with crushed crackers and peanuts.

INGREDIENTS

Prawns (shrimps)	500 g (1 lb 1½ oz), peeled, leaving tails intact, deveined
Chilli powder	1 tsp
Salt	½ tsp + 1 pinch
Spring onions (scallions)	50 g (1¾ oz), chopped
Cooking oil	100 ml (3½ fl oz)
Minced garlic	1 tsp
Minced onion	1 tsp
Pork thigh	300 g (11 oz), thinly sliced
Pork stock	from boiling 1 kg (2 lb 3 oz) pork bones in 2 litres (64 fl oz / 8 cups) water for 1–2 hours
Fish sauce	½ tsp + 2 Tbsp
Chicken seasoning powder	½ tsp
Fresh flat yellow noodles	500 g (1 lb 1½ oz)
Bean sprouts	100 g (3½ oz)
Mint leaves	50 g (1¾ oz)
Roasted sesame cracker	1, 30 × 30 cm (12 × 12 in), coarsely crushed
Skinned peanuts	100 g (3½ oz), roasted and coarsely ground
Red chillies	2, sliced
Limes	3, quartered

METHOD

- Put prawns into a bowl. Add $^1/_2$ tsp each of chilli powder and salt and spring onions. Mix well and set aside.

- Heat oil in a pot. Fry garlic and onion until golden over medium heat. Add remaining chilli powder and pork slices. Stir-fry for 5 minutes. Add prawns and stir-fry for another 5 minutes.

- Add stock and bring to the boil. Skim scum from liquid surface. Season with 1 pinch salt, $^1/_2$ tsp fish sauce and seasoning powder.

- Put desired amount of noodles and bean sprouts into individual serving bowls. Top with mint leaves. Ladle boiling soup over, then sprinkle on crushed crackers and ground peanuts. Serve hot with remaining fish sauce, chilli and lime on the side.

peanut and sago dessert Serves 4–6

With green beans, peanuts, sago and wood ear fungus, this dessert has a delightful variety of soft and crunchy textures.

INGREDIENTS

Green (mung) beans	300 g (11 oz), soaked in water for 1 hour, or until softened then rub off and discard skins
Peanuts	100 g (3$^1/_2$ oz), soaked in water for 1 hour and drained
Sugar	200 g (7 oz)
Water	2 litres (64 fl oz / 8 cups)
Sago	50 g (1$^3/_4$ oz), soaked in water for 1 hour, or until softened
Dried wood ear fungus	50 g (1$^3/_4$ oz), soaked in water to soften, then finely shredded
Coconut cream	200 ml (6$^1/_2$ fl oz)
Screwpine (pandan) leaves	4, washed and dried, or $^1/_2$ tsp vanilla essence
Salt	$^1/_2$ tsp

METHOD

- Steam skinless green beans for about 5 minutes or until cooked through, but not soggy.

- Put peanuts in a pot. Add sufficient water to cover, then boil for about 20 minutes or until softened. Drain peanuts well, then transfer to a bowl. Add sugar and mix.

- Bring 2 litres (64 fl oz / 8 cups) water to the boil in a large pot. Add soaked sago and cook for 10 minutes, or until sago becomes clear.

- Add all remaining ingredients and return to the boil, then turn off heat.

- Serve hot or cold.

sweet yam dessert Serves 4–6

Similar to but starchier than the mango and sticky rice of Thai fame, this dessert is easy to prepare and is a tasty way to wrap up any meal.

INGREDIENTS

Water	2 litres (64 fl oz / 8 cups)
Glutinous rice	250 g (9 oz), washed and soaked in water for 1–2 hours
Salt	1/2 tsp
Sugar	300 g (11 oz)
Yam (taro)	500 g (1 lb 1 1/2 oz), peeled and cut into bite-size cubes
Screwpine (pandan) leaves	4, washed, dried and tied together to form a bunch, or 1/2 tsp vanilla essence
Coconut milk	300 ml (10 fl oz / 1 1/4 cups)

METHOD

- Bring water to the boil in a pot. Add glutinous rice and cook for 20 minutes, or until liquid is no longer visible from the top.

- Add salt and half the sugar, then cook until both are completely dissolved.

- Add yam, remaining sugar and screwpine leaves or vanilla essence. Do not stir. Cook over low heat for 15 minutes, or until yam cubes are cooked.

- Mix in coconut milk, then remove from heat and leave to cool.

- Alternatively, coconut milk can be served separately alongside dessert. For this, bring coconut milk to the boil, then add a solution of corn flour (cornstarch) and water to thicken.

- Serve in small bowls at room temperature.

tapioca cake Makes one 20–25-cm (8–10-in) cake

As delicate as much of Vietnamese cuisine is, this cake is mildly fragrant from the coconut cream and not overbearingly sweet.

INGREDIENTS

Tapioca	I kg (2 lb 3 oz), peeled and cut into small pieces, then blended until fine and pasty
Coconut cream	200 ml (6^1/$_2$ fl oz)
Sweetened condensed milk	3 tsp
Vanilla essence	^{1}/$_2$ tsp
Sugar	100 g (3^1/$_2$ oz)
Salt	^{1}/$_2$ tsp
Butter	50 g (1^3/$_4$ oz)

METHOD

- Put tapioca paste into a cloth bag or fine strainer. Squeeze firmly to drain out excess liquid. Use about 650 g (1 lb 6^1/$_2$ oz) tapioca paste to make cake. Reserve and refrigerate any remainder for future use.

- Put tapioca paste into a large bowl. Mix in coconut cream, condensed milk, vanilla essence, sugar, salt and half the butter.

- Melt remaining butter and use it to grease the base of a 20–25 cm (8–10-in) round metal cake tin. Press tapioca paste into tin.

- Bake in an oven preheated to 180°C (350°F) for about 15 minutes, or until surface is golden brown.

- Remove cake from oven and leave to cool. Turn out cooled cake from tin, then slice and serve.

fresh aloe vera with green bean soup Serves 4–6

Cooked aloe vera may not taste of very much, but they leave a lightly tangy after-taste that is refreshing and welcome to a laden palate.

INGREDIENTS

Split green (mung) beans	300 g (11 oz), leave skins on if attached
Dried lotus seeds (optional)	100 g (3¹/₂ oz), or fresh ones if available
Water	1.5 litres (48 fl oz / 6 cups)
Sugar	100 g (3¹/₂ oz), or to taste
Aloe vera leaves	2, peeled and sliced or cubed

METHOD

- Soak green beans in water for 2 hours and drain before use. Do not discard skins if beans were not skinned.

- If using dried lotus seeds, soak in water for 2 hours, then drain before use. Fresh lotus seeds do not need soaking.

- Boil soaked lotus seeds, if used, in plenty of water until soft, then drain. Fresh lotus seeds do not need boiling.

- Combine lotus seeds, green beans and 1.5 litres (48 fl oz / 6 cups) water in a pot. Cook for about 20 minutes, or until lotus seeds and green beans are cooked through and soft.

- Add sugar to taste, then add aloe vera pieces. Remove from heat, ladle into individual serving bowls and serve.

black-eyed peas in glutinous rice Serves 4–6

Another filling end to a meal, this substantial dessert is flavoured by a fragrant combination of coconut milk and vanilla essence.

INGREDIENTS

Black-eyed peas	300 g (11 oz), soaked in cold water for 3 hours, then drained
Bicarbonate of (baking) soda	1 tsp
Water	1.75 litres (56 fl oz / 7 cups)
Glutinous rice	250 g (9 oz)
Sugar	350 g (12$\frac{1}{2}$ oz)
Coconut milk	125 ml (4 fl oz / $\frac{1}{2}$ cup)
Vanilla essence	$\frac{1}{2}$ tsp

METHOD

• Combine peas, bicarbonate of soda and 1 litre (32 fl oz / 4 cups) water in a pot. Bring to the boil and sustain for about 1 hour. Do not over boil.

• When peas are soft, but not broken, remove from heat, drain and set aside.

• Rinse rice grains twice. Cook rice in remaining water over low heat for about 45 minutes, stirring frequently. When rice liquid is mostly evaporated, add boiled peas and cook for 20 minutes. Add remaining ingredients, mix well and cook for another 20 minutes.

• When dessert is thickened and consistent in texture, remove from heat. Serve.

weights and measures

Quantities for this book are given in Metric, Imperial and American (spoon and cup) measures. Standard spoon and cup measurements used are: 1 tsp = 5 ml, 1 Tbsp = 15 ml, 1 cup = 250 ml. All measures are level unless otherwise stated.

Liquid And Volume Measures

Metric	Imperial	American
5 ml	$1/6$ fl oz	1 teaspoon
10 ml	$1/3$ fl oz	1 dessertspoon
15 ml	$1/2$ fl oz	1 tablespoon
60 ml	2 fl oz	$1/4$ cup (4 tablespoons)
85 ml	$2^1/2$ fl oz	$1/3$ cup
90 ml	3 fl oz	$3/8$ cup (6 tablespoons)
125 ml	4 fl oz	$1/2$ cup
180 ml	6 fl oz	$3/4$ cup
250 ml	8 fl oz	1 cup
300 ml	10 fl oz ($1/2$ pint)	$1^1/4$ cups
375 ml	12 fl oz	$1^1/2$ cups
435 ml	14 fl oz	$1^3/4$ cups
500 ml	16 fl oz	2 cups
625 ml	20 fl oz (1 pint)	$2^1/2$ cups
750 ml	24 fl oz ($1^1/5$ pints)	3 cups
1 litre	32 fl oz ($1^3/5$ pints)	4 cups
1.25 litres	40 fl oz (2 pints)	5 cups
1.5 litres	48 fl oz ($2^2/5$ pints)	6 cups
2.5 litres	80 fl oz (4 pints)	10 cups

Dry Measures

Metric	Imperial
30 grams	1 ounce
45 grams	$1^1/2$ ounces
55 grams	2 ounces
70 grams	$2^1/2$ ounces
85 grams	3 ounces
100 grams	$3^1/2$ ounces
110 grams	4 ounces
125 grams	$4^1/2$ ounces
140 grams	5 ounces
280 grams	10 ounces
450 grams	16 ounces (1 pound)
500 grams	1 pound, $1^1/2$ ounces
700 grams	$1^1/2$ pounds
800 grams	$1^3/4$ pounds
1 kilogram	2 pounds, 3 ounces
1.5 kilograms	3 pounds, $4^1/2$ ounces
2 kilograms	4 pounds, 6 ounces

Length

Metric	Imperial
0.5 cm	$1/4$ inch
1 cm	$1/2$ inch
1.5 cm	$3/4$ inch
2.5 cm	1 inch

Oven Temperature

	°C	°F	Gas Regulo
Very slow	120	250	1
Slow	150	300	2
Moderately slow	160	325	3
Moderate	180	350	4
Moderately hot	190/200	375/400	5/6
Hot	210/220	410/425	6/7
Very hot	230	450	8
Super hot	250/290	475/550	9/10

Abbreviation

tsp	teaspoon
Tbsp	tablespoon
g	gram
kg	kilogram
ml	millilitre